The Magic and Mystery of Northern Lights

Daniel Fankhauser

scrAibs.com

Contents

Prologue 4

Chapter 1: The Cosmic Dance 6

Chapter 2: Best Spots to See the Lights....................................9

Chapter 3: Chasing the Lights..14

Chapter 4: Unexpected Places 20

Chapter 5: When and How to Catch 25

Chapter 6: Photography of the Northern Lights 31

Chapter 7: The Myths and Mysteries 38

Chapter 8: The Future of Auroras 43

Chapter 9: Common Misconceptions 49

Chapter 10: The Call of the Northern Lights............................55

Chapter 11: Journey Through Art and Culture 60

Chapter 12: The Auroras on other Planets 63

Chapter 13: The Science Behind the Spectacle 66

Chapter 14: The Impact on Mental Health 71

Conclusion: The Universal Dance 76

Epilogue 79

Prologue

In the deep stillness of the Arctic night, there's a moment when the world feels like it's holding its breath. The stars above are sharp and bright, scattered across the sky like shards of ice. The air is crisp and cold, and the silence is profound, broken only by the distant sigh of the wind. You're standing in the heart of winter, where the sun barely rises, and the night stretches on endlessly. It's a place where time seems to slow, where the natural world takes on an ancient, timeless quality.

And then, just when you've given up hope, it happens.

A faint glow appears on the horizon, barely noticeable at first, like a wisp of smoke curling through the air. But as you watch, the light grows stronger, brighter, and soon, it begins to move. It swirls and stretches across the sky in waves of green and purple, like a painter's brush sweeping across a canvas. The sky is no longer just a backdrop—it has come alive, pulsing and shifting as if in response to some cosmic rhythm.

The northern lights, the aurora borealis, are unlike anything else on Earth. They are a dance of light and time, a meeting of the forces of the sun and the Earth, creating a spectacle that has inspired awe and wonder for millennia. For the ancient people who lived under these skies, the lights were more than just a natural phenomenon—they were messages from the gods, omens of things to come, or the spirits of ancestors playing in the heavens.

Even today, in our age of technology and science, the northern lights retain their magic. They remind us that, despite all we've learned about the universe, there are still things that can take our breath away. They are a reminder of the beauty that exists beyond our reach, and of the mysteries that still linger in the night sky.

This book is a journey into the world of the northern lights—a journey through science, myth, and wonder. It's a guide for those who want to understand the auroras, for those who dream of seeing them, and for those who have already stood beneath their shimmering glow. We'll explore how the lights form, where and when to see them, and the stories they've inspired across cultures and centuries.

But more than that, this book is a celebration of the auroras as a symbol of our connection to the universe. Whether you're standing in the Arctic wilderness or watching from your own backyard during a rare southern display, the northern lights are a reminder that the world is full of wonders—if we only stop to look.

So, let's begin our journey. The lights are waiting.

Chapter 1: The Cosmic Dance

Imagine standing in the deep silence of a frozen wilderness. The stars above you are sharp and clear, scattered across the vast black sky like diamonds. There's no city glow, no sounds but the whisper of the wind moving over the snow. Then, it happens—at first just a faint shimmer, like someone lightly brushing their hand across the heavens. But in moments, the faint glimmer grows, stretching like a giant ribbon. Suddenly, the sky is alive. Green, purple, and pink lights surge and pulse, like a cosmic heartbeat. You feel as though you've been let in on a celestial secret—the aurora borealis.

The northern lights, or aurora borealis, are one of nature's most incredible displays. They have captivated humans for centuries, their origins a mystery until relatively recently. Now, thanks to scientific discovery, we understand that this ethereal phenomenon is a result of solar winds colliding with Earth's magnetic field. But knowing the science doesn't make them any less magical.

The story of the northern lights starts with the sun. Solar flares— massive bursts of energy—explode from the surface of the sun, sending particles streaming through space. These particles, mainly electrons and protons, are caught by the Earth's magnetic field when they reach our planet. The particles are drawn toward the magnetic poles, where they interact with the gases in our atmosphere. This interaction releases energy in the form of light—creating the auroras that dance across polar skies.

But this isn't just any light show. The colors we see in the northern lights come from different gases. When these solar particles collide with oxygen high in the Earth's atmosphere, the lights glow green, the most common color. If they interact with nitrogen, they can turn purple, red, or pink. The higher the solar activity, the more intense the colors and the more frequent the displays.

This cosmic event, born of the sun's violent energy and Earth's protective shield, plays out silently in the sky, offering those who witness it a fleeting glimpse of a world beyond our everyday reality.

But why do these lights only occur near the poles? The Earth's magnetic field acts like a giant funnel, guiding solar particles toward the North and South Poles. This is why the aurora borealis is mostly visible in high-latitude areas, such as Norway, Canada, Alaska, and northern Russia. These regions lie beneath the "auroral oval"—an area where the interaction between solar particles and Earth's atmosphere is most intense. On rare occasions, when solar storms are particularly strong, the auroras can be seen further south, delighting skywatchers in places like Ohio, New York, and even Texas.

The northern lights have captivated humans for thousands of years, inspiring legends and myths in cultures all over the world. To the ancient Vikings, the lights were thought to be reflections of the Valkyries' armor as they guided fallen warriors to Valhalla. In Inuit mythology, the auroras were believed to be the spirits of ancestors, playing a game with a walrus skull high in the heavens. Even today, the lights hold a special place in the hearts of those who live in regions where they are a regular occurrence.

While we now understand the scientific reasons behind the northern lights, there's still something deeply mysterious and enchanting about them. You can know everything about the solar particles, the magnetic field, and the physics involved, but standing beneath a sky ablaze with color still feels like witnessing a miracle.

And that's the magic of the auroras—they remind us how small we are in the grand scheme of the universe, and how much there is that we still don't know. Even in an age where we've sent probes to the outer edges of our solar system, the northern lights remain a spectacle of nature that fills us with wonder.

So, as you begin your journey into the world of the northern lights, remember that you're not just learning about science. You're becoming part of a tradition—a long history of humans looking up at the sky and being awestruck by something that, for all its mystery, makes us feel connected to the universe. And while you may now know the science, the next time you find yourself beneath an aurora-filled sky, let the magic take over.

Chapter 2: Best Spots to See the Lights

The northern lights are as elusive as they are beautiful. You can't just drive out any night and expect the sky to explode into a vivid dance of greens and purples. No, aurora chasing is a careful game of patience, timing, and sometimes, pure luck. There's a reason it's often called "chasing" the lights—you might wait for hours, or even days, in some of the most remote and coldest places on Earth. But when the sky finally opens up and the auroras appear, the wait is always worth it.

Where, then, should you go if you want to maximize your chances of catching this extraordinary natural wonder? While the lights can sometimes make rare appearances in unexpected places, there are a handful of locations that offer your best shot at witnessing the northern lights in all their glory. These are the places where magic meets the Earth, where the aurora borealis appears most frequently and brilliantly.

Tromsø, Norway – The Gateway to the Arctic

Tromsø, located high above the Arctic Circle in Norway, is often called the "Gateway to the Arctic." This small city has earned its reputation as one of the best places on Earth to see the northern lights. The unique geography of Tromsø places it directly beneath the auroral oval, which means that even when solar activity is low, your chances of catching a display here are high.

But Tromsø offers more than just the lights. Picture yourself standing on a frozen fjord, the crisp night air biting at your skin, with snow-covered mountains looming in the background. The auroras aren't just something you look up at—they become part of the entire landscape, reflecting off the ice and water around you, making the world feel otherworldly.

For many travelers, Tromsø is more than just a destination to see the auroras. It's an adventure. You can take a husky sled ride through the wilderness, stay in a traditional Sami tent, or even board a cruise along Norway's stunning coastline, all while waiting for the northern lights to make their appearance.

Fairbanks, Alaska – The Northern Light Capital

In Alaska, the aurora borealis feels like a part of daily life. Fairbanks, located deep in the interior of the state, is renowned for its incredible northern lights displays. The city sits beneath a particularly active part of the auroral oval, which makes it one of the top places in the United States to view the lights.

But Fairbanks offers something that few other places can: convenience. Unlike many remote northern lights destinations, Fairbanks is easily accessible by plane and has a wide range of accommodations. You don't have to trek into the wilderness to see the lights here. On a clear night, you can simply step outside and look up, and there's a good chance the auroras will be dancing overhead.

Of course, if you want the full Alaskan experience, there are plenty of options to get out into nature. You can book a stay at one of the many wilderness lodges around Fairbanks, where you'll be far from any light pollution and have the best possible view of the sky. Or, for a truly unique adventure, take a dip in the Chena Hot Springs, where you can soak in warm waters under a canopy of northern lights.

Abisko, Sweden – A Window into the Sky

Abisko is a small village in the Swedish Lapland, and it's one of the best-kept secrets in northern lights tourism. The area is famous for its clear skies—something that's not always easy to find in the Arctic regions, where clouds can quickly ruin your aurora-watching plans.

The magic of Abisko comes from its unique geography. The village sits in a valley surrounded by mountains, creating what's known as the "blue hole" effect. This is a pocket of clear skies that stays relatively cloud-free, even when the surrounding areas are covered in clouds. For aurora chasers, this is a huge advantage, as it means you have a higher chance of seeing the lights on any given night.

Abisko is also home to the Aurora Sky Station, a mountaintop observatory specifically designed for watching the northern lights. Take a chairlift up the mountain, and you'll be greeted with one of the most spectacular views in the world— unobstructed, 360-degree vistas of the Arctic sky. On a good night, the entire horizon can be lit up with auroras, making it feel like you're floating in the middle of a cosmic display.

Reykjavik, Iceland – Auroras and Adventure

Iceland is a land of fire and ice, where glaciers meet volcanic landscapes, and waterfalls tumble into the ocean. It's a place where nature feels alive and untamed, and that's exactly how the northern lights feel when you see them here.

Reykjavik, the country's capital, is one of the most accessible places to start your northern lights adventure. On clear nights, the lights can often be seen just outside the city, but for the best experience, it's worth venturing out to the more remote areas of the country.

Imagine standing on the edge of a black sanc beach, the cold wind whipping through your hair, and watching the sky above you come alive with shifting colors. Or picture yourself soaking in one of Iceland's many natural hot springs, with the northern lights shimmering overhead. In Iceland, the lights are not just a skyward event; they become part of the dramatic landscape around you.

Yukon, Canada – Wilderness and Wonder

In Canada's Yukon Territory, the auroras are a regular part of life during the long, dark winters. Whitehorse, the territory's capital, is an excellent base for aurora watching, with a wide range of outdoor activities to keep you entertained while you wait for night to fall.

But to truly experience the magic of the northern lights in the Yukon, it's worth heading out to one of the many wilderness lodges that dot the region. Here, under some of the darkest skies in the world, you'll have front-row seats to one of nature's greatest spectacles. Picture yourself sitting in front of a roaring fire, with nothing but snow-covered trees and mountains around you, as the northern lights fill the sky with their ethereal glow.

Unexpected Auroras – When the Lights Surprise Us

While places like Norway, Alaska, and Iceland are famous for their auroras, the northern lights don't always stick to the script. Sometimes, a powerful solar storm will cause the lights to appear in places much further south than usual, giving people in cities like Ohio, New York, and even Texas a rare chance to witness the magic.

These events are always unpredictable, but thanks to advances in technology, it's easier than ever to stay informed. Apps and websites now allow you to track auroral activity in real-time, giving you alerts when the lights might be visible in your area. Imagine receiving a notification on your phone that says, "Northern lights visible in New York tonight," and rushing outside to catch a glimpse of the auroras in a place where they're rarely seen.

These surprise displays often cause a buzz on social media, with people sharing their excitement at seeing the lights in unexpected places. Whether you're in a city like Chicago or a small town in Pennsylvania, the thrill of spotting the northern lights is always the same.

The Ultimate Aurora Adventure

For those who are serious about chasing the northern lights, planning a trip to one of these prime aurora-viewing locations is a must. Whether you're standing on a frozen fjord in Norway, soaking in hot springs in Iceland, or huddling around a campfire in the Yukon wilderness, the experience of seeing the auroras will stay with you forever.

But wherever you choose to go, remember this: the northern lights are fickle, and they don't appear on demand. There will be nights when the sky stays stubbornly dark, and you might wonder if the trip was worth it. But when the lights finally do appear—when the sky opens up and the auroras begin their dance—you'll know it was worth every second of waiting.

The northern lights are a reminder of the beauty and unpredictability of nature. They show us that even in a world filled with technology and certainty, there are still things that can surprise and astonish us. So, bundle up, head out into the night, and keep your eyes on the sky. You never know when the magic might happen.

Chapter 3: Chasing the Lights

The northern lights are unpredictable by nature, but that doesn't mean you have to rely solely on luck to see them. In fact, modern technology and science have made it easier than ever to track and predict when and where the auroras will appear. But even with all the tools at your disposal, there's something thrilling about the chase. The northern lights, after all, are one of nature's last true mysteries, and part of their magic is that they never appear quite the same way twice.

In this chapter, we'll dive into the art of chasing auroras—how to read forecasts, which apps and websites can help you track them, and what you need to know to maximize your chances of being in the right place at the right time. Whether you're planning a trip to the Arctic Circle or hoping for a rare display in your hometown, understanding how to predict auroral activity is key to catching the northern lights in action.

At the heart of every aurora is the sun. The northern lights wouldn't exist without solar energy, and the intensity of the display depends on how much energy the sun is throwing our way at any given moment.

The sun is constantly releasing streams of charged particles, known as the **solar wind**, which travel millions of miles through space. When these particles collide with Earth's magnetic field, they're guided toward the poles, where they interact with the gases in our atmosphere, creating the light show we know as the aurora borealis.

But the sun doesn't always behave the same way. Sometimes, it releases more particles than usual in the form of **solar flares** or **coronal mass ejections (CMEs)**. These events send massive bursts of energy into space, which can significantly increase the chances of auroras on Earth. When a CME hits our planet's magnetic field, it can trigger a **geomagnetic storm**, which supercharges the auroras and makes them visible over a much wider area than usual. This is when you might hear reports of auroras appearing in places as far south as Texas or California.

The key to chasing the northern lights is to understand the relationship between solar activity and geomagnetic storms. The stronger the storm, the better your chances of seeing the lights—and the more vibrant and widespread the display will be.

One of the most important tools for aurora chasers is the **KP index**. The KP index is a measure of geomagnetic activity, and it's expressed as a number on a scale from 0 to 9. The higher the number, the stronger the geomagnetic storm—and the more likely you are to see auroras.

- A KP index of **0 to 2**: Low geomagnetic activity. Auroras are unlikely to be visible outside the polar regions.

- A KP index of **3 to 4**: Moderate geomagnetic activity. Auroras may be visible in northern latitudes such as Canada, Alaska, and Scandinavia.

- A KP index of **5 or higher**: High geomagnetic activity. This is where things get exciting. When the KP index hits 5 or above, auroras can be visible much further south than usual, possibly in places like the northern United States, the UK, or even central Europe.

- A KP index of **7 or higher**: A major geomagnetic storm. This is when auroras can reach areas that almost never see them, such as the southern United States or southern parts of Europe.

Tracking the KP index is essential for aurora chasers because it gives you an indication of how likely the northern lights are to appear in your location. Several websites and apps offer real-time KP index updates, so you can monitor conditions and be ready when a storm hits.

Thanks to modern technology, chasing the northern lights has never been easier. There are a variety of apps, websites, and tools available that provide real-time data on auroral activity, giving you the best chance of catching a display. Here are some of the most popular and reliable resources for aurora hunters:

1. **Aurora Forecast by the NOAA (National Oceanic and Atmospheric Administration)**: This website offers detailed forecasts of auroral activity, including the KP index, solar wind data, and geomagnetic storm predictions. It's a go-to resource for anyone serious about chasing auroras.

2. **My Aurora Forecast & Alerts (App)**: This popular app gives you real-time alerts when auroras are visible in your area. It also provides a detailed forecast, including KP index updates, cloud cover information, and a map showing where auroras are most likely to be visible.

3. **Aurora Alerts (App)**: Similar to My Aurora Forecast, this app offers real-time alerts and forecasts based on the KP index. It's easy to use and a favorite among aurora chasers.

4. **SpaceWeatherLive.com**: A comprehensive website that provides up-to-the-minute information on solar activity, geomagnetic storms, and auroral forecasts. It's a great resource for anyone looking to dive deep into the science behind auroras.

5. **Aurora Service (Website)**: This site offers real-time auroral activity maps, KP index updates, and forecasts for different regions around the world.

Using these tools, you can plan your aurora-watching trips with a higher degree of confidence. The key is to stay informed and be ready to act when conditions are right. If the KP index spikes and the forecast looks promising, it's time to grab your coat and head outside.

Once you have the tools to track auroral activity, the next step is knowing when and where to watch. While the KP index is the primary indicator of geomagnetic activity, there are other factors that can affect your chances of seeing the northern lights.

1. Clear Skies are Essential: No matter how strong the auroral activity is, you won't see anything if the sky is cloudy. This is why many aurora chasers head to regions known for their clear, dark skies, such as Abisko in Sweden or the Yukon in Canada. Before heading out, check local weather forecasts to ensure you'll have clear skies for aurora viewing.

2. Dark Nights are Best: The northern lights are best seen in the darkest hours of the night. If you're too close to city lights, or if the moon is particularly bright, it can wash out the auroras. That's why it's best to head to remote areas with minimal light pollution, such as national parks or wilderness areas.

3. Winter is Prime Aurora Season: While auroras can technically happen any time of year, they're most visible during the long, dark winter months. The best time to see the northern lights is between September and March, when the nights are longest and the skies are darkest.

While the northern lights can technically be seen in any location with sufficient geomagnetic activity, some regions are better suited for aurora viewing than others. These "aurora hotspots" are located directly beneath the auroral oval, making them prime locations for catching frequent and intense displays.

- **Tromsø, Norway**: This Arctic city is one of the best places in the world to see the northern lights. Located beneath the auroral oval, Tromsø offers frequent aurora sightings during the winter months.

- **Fairbanks, Alaska**: Another popular destination for aurora hunters, Fairbanks is located in the heart of Alaska, where the northern lights are visible on most clear winter nights.

- **Yellowknife, Canada**: The capital of Canada's Northwest Territories, Yellowknife is famous for its dark skies and frequent auroral displays. It's one of the best places in North America to see the northern lights.

- **Reykjavik, Iceland**: Iceland's unique geography and low light pollution make it a popular destination for aurora hunters. While Reykjavik itself offers good aurora views, many travelers venture into the Icelandic countryside for a more immersive experience.

- **Abisko, Sweden**: Known for its clear skies and minimal cloud cover, Abisko is a hidden gem for aurora chasers. The surrounding mountains create a "blue hole" effect, keeping the skies clear even when nearby areas are cloudy.

Chasing the northern lights requires patience, but the payoff is worth it. There will be nights when the KP index looks promising, the skies are clear, and yet, the auroras remain hidden. It's easy to get frustrated after hours of standing in the cold, staring at a dark sky. But then, just when you're about to give up, it happens—the first shimmer of green appears on the horizon, quickly growing into a swirling, dancing curtain of light.

This is the magic of aurora chasing. It's not just about the lights themselves; it's about the anticipation, the buildup, and the joy of finally seeing the sky come alive. When you do catch the northern lights, it feels like a gift—something special that can't be controlled or predicted with certainty.

So, when you're out there chasing the lights, remember that part of the adventure is the waiting. The northern lights don't perform on command, but when they do appear, they'll make all the waiting and preparation worthwhile.

Chapter 4: Unexpected Places

For most people, witnessing the northern lights is something reserved for the far northern corners of the Earth—places like Alaska, Norway, and Canada, where the aurora borealis regularly graces the skies. But occasionally, the lights decide to surprise us, showing up in places far removed from their typical domain. Imagine walking through the streets of Chicago, Los Angeles, or even Dallas, only to look up and see the sky awash in ghostly green and violet.

It sounds like a scene out of a movie, but it's real. And it happens more often than you might think, especially during periods of intense solar activity. When the sun throws a particularly strong geomagnetic storm our way, the auroras can stretch far beyond their usual boundaries, creating rare opportunities for skywatchers in unlikely places. This chapter will explore the stories, the science, and the excitement behind seeing the northern lights in cities where they don't normally belong.

Before we dive into the specific places where the auroras have made surprise appearances, let's talk about what makes these extraordinary sightings possible: geomagnetic storms. As we learned in the previous chapter, the aurora borealis is powered by solar energy, specifically the solar wind that streams from the sun toward Earth. Most of the time, this solar wind creates beautiful light shows around the polar regions, where Earth's magnetic field is strongest. But every so often, the sun unleashes something even more powerful—a coronal mass ejection (CME).

A CME is a massive burst of solar wind and magnetic fields rising above the solar corona. When this giant wave of energy reaches Earth, it can cause a geomagnetic storm. These storms supercharge the auroras, not only making them more intense but also pushing them much further south than usual. The stronger the storm, the further from the poles the auroras can be seen.

The strength of a geomagnetic storm is measured on the KP index, a scale from 0 to 9. For northern lights to be visible in cities like New York or Chicago, the KP index typically needs to reach 6 or higher. In extreme cases, with a KP index of 7 or above, the auroras can stretch as far south as Texas or Florida.

Now, let's explore some of the most memorable moments when the northern lights decided to make surprise appearances over major cities and unexpected locations. These are the nights when people in places far from the Arctic Circle glanced up and witnessed something extraordinary.

1. The Chicago Surprise: Auroras Over the Windy City

Chicago may be known for its iconic skyline, deep-dish pizza, and bitter winters, but it's not a city where people expect to see the northern lights. That changed on the night of March 23, 2023, when a powerful geomagnetic storm sent auroras cascading over the Great Lakes region, including Chicago.

For many residents, it was a complete shock. As the lights began to shimmer in the sky, social media exploded with photos and videos from people who had never dreamed they'd see the northern lights from their own backyard. The auroras in Chicago that night appeared in soft greens and purples, creating a surreal backdrop to the city's skyline. For those who were lucky enough to be outside when it happened, it was a moment they would never forget.

2. New York City: A Rare Display Over the Big Apple

New York is often called "the city that never sleeps," but even in this bustling metropolis, the sky doesn't often get much attention. Between the bright lights of Times Square and the towering skyscrapers, the northern lights are not something you'd expect to see here. But on rare occasions, when the geomagnetic storms are strong enough, the auroras make an appearance even in the Big Apple.

One of the most famous occurrences took place in September 1941, when a particularly powerful solar storm caused auroras to appear over New York City. People spilled out of their homes and apartments to gaze at the unusual sight, and newspapers the next day marveled at the spectacle. Since then, there have been a few other instances when the auroras have graced the skies over New York, but each time it happens, it feels like a once-in-a-lifetime event.

3. Texas and the Southern U.S.: A Shocking Display

Perhaps the most unlikely place to witness the northern lights is in the southern United States, where the warm climates and southern latitude make auroras a rare sight indeed. But during the historic geomagnetic storm of October 29-30, 2003, the lights were visible as far south as **Texas, Florida,** and even **Mexico.** This event, known as the **Halloween Storm,** was one of the most powerful solar storms on record, and it sent auroras cascading across skies where they had never been seen before.

In Texas, the lights appeared as faint, glowing clouds of red and green, an eerie and mesmerizing sight against the usual backdrop of stars and warm southern air. For residents who witnessed it, the event was so unusual that many initially thought it was a fire in the distance or an unusual weather phenomenon.

4. Los Angeles and the West Coast: Lights Over the City of Angels

On rare occasions, the northern lights have even been spotted over California. During periods of strong geomagnetic activity, residents of cities like **Los Angeles** and **San Francisco** have reported seeing faint glows of green and red on the northern horizon. While these displays are usually less intense than those seen in higher latitudes, they are no less exciting for those who live in these unexpected aurora hotspots.

One notable sighting occurred in March 1989, during a powerful solar storm that caused auroras to be visible over much of the northern United States and as far south as California. In Los Angeles, the lights appeared as a faint red glow, blending into the urban haze but still distinct enough to cause a stir among those who happened to glance up at the right moment.

5. Auroras in Europe: When the Lights Travel South

It's not just North America that experiences surprise auroras. In Europe, the northern lights have made appearances in places like **London**, **Paris**, and even as far south as **Rome**. During major solar storms, auroras have been spotted over the skies of southern Europe, creating a rare and magical sight for those lucky enough to witness it.

One of the most famous aurora sightings in Europe occurred in November 2003, during the same geomagnetic storm that caused auroras in Texas and Mexico. In parts of southern France and Italy, the lights appeared in vivid shades of red and green, lighting up the skies in a way that few had ever seen before.

While it's impossible to predict exactly when and where the northern lights will make these surprise appearances, there are a few steps you can take to increase your chances of catching them the next time they venture south.

1. **Keep an Eye on the KP Index**: As mentioned earlier, the KP index is your best guide to predicting auroral activity. If the KP index hits 5 or above, it's worth heading outside and checking the skies, especially if you live in a location that doesn't typically see auroras.

2. **Follow Aurora Alerts**: There are several apps and websites that offer real-time aurora alerts, which will notify you if there's a chance of seeing the northern

lights in your area. These alerts can give you a heads-up when conditions are right for a surprise auroral display.

3. **Get Away from City Lights**: Even in cities where the auroras aren't expected, light pollution can make it difficult to see them if they do appear. If you get an aurora alert and live in a major city, consider driving to a nearby park or rural area with less light pollution for a better view.

4. **Be Prepared for the Unexpected**: The magic of the northern lights is that they often appear when you least expect them. Keep an open mind and be ready to embrace the moment when the lights do make an appearance. Even if you don't live in a northern region, you might just be lucky enough to catch a glimpse of one of nature's most incredible shows.

There's something uniquely thrilling about seeing the northern lights in a place where they don't belong. It feels like a special kind of magic, as if the universe has decided to put on a show just for you. Whether you're in Chicago, Texas, or Los Angeles, the experience of seeing the auroras in an unexpected location is a reminder that even in the most familiar places, there's always room for surprise and wonder.

So, the next time you hear about a geomagnetic storm or get an aurora alert for your area, don't hesitate. Step outside, look up, and see if the northern lights have come to visit. You never know when the sky might decide to put on a show.

Chapter 5: When and How to Catch

There's a certain romance to aurora chasing, a kind of slow-burn thrill that builds as you wait for the perfect moment. Whether you're standing in the frozen wilderness of northern Norway or in a quiet field in Michigan, the anticipation of catching the northern lights can feel like waiting for a cosmic gift. But timing is everything when it comes to auroras. Unlike a meteor shower or a predictable astronomical event, the northern lights don't have a fixed schedule. They come and go on their own terms, dancing across the sky at their whim. That said, if you know where and when to look, you can dramatically increase your chances of catching the show.

In this chapter, we'll dive into the best times to see the northern lights, how long they usually last, and the different factors that influence visibility. Whether you're planning a trip to one of the aurora hotspots around the world or hoping for a rare sighting in your own backyard, understanding the patterns of the auroras will help you prepare for your own celestial adventure.

While the aurora borealis is technically visible all year round, the best time to see it is during the long, dark nights of winter. The further north you go, the shorter the days become in the winter months, giving you more time to catch the lights in action.

For most aurora viewing locations, the prime aurora season runs from September to March. During these months, the skies are dark enough for the auroras to be visible for extended periods, and the solar activity that drives the lights tends to peak. Let's break down the aurora season by months:

1. September and October: Early fall is one of the best times to see the northern lights because the nights are long enough, but not yet brutally cold. In places like Alaska, Norway, and Canada, the auroras start to become more active as the summer sun fades. There's

something magical about standing in the crisp autumn air, watching the northern lights flicker through the first signs of winter.

2. November to January: The heart of winter brings the longest nights and, in some places, near-total darkness for days or even weeks. In regions like northern Norway, Iceland, and parts of Canada, the aurora borealis can be visible for hours at a time during this period, since there's no daylight to wash them out. These months also tend to be the coldest, so while the viewing is excellent, it's important to be prepared for extreme winter conditions.

3. February and March: As winter begins to ease, auroras remain active, and the days start to grow longer again. By March, the skies still get plenty dark, but the temperatures are slightly more tolerable for those who aren't fans of deep freezes. Solar activity also tends to increase around this time, leading to more frequent auroral displays.

While the winter months offer the best conditions for aurora viewing, some locations still have excellent chances of seeing the lights in late summer, particularly during August and early September. In places like northern Alaska and the Yukon, where the midnight sun lingers into late summer, the auroras begin to appear as the nights grow darker.

Once you've narrowed down the right season, the next question is: what time of night should you be looking? The aurora borealis tends to be most active between 10 p.m. and 2 a.m. local time, but this isn't a hard-and-fast rule. Auroras can appear at any time during the night, especially if the geomagnetic activity is strong.

One trick used by many aurora chasers is to set up camp outside early in the evening and keep an eye on the sky until after midnight. This way, you give yourself the maximum window of opportunity to catch the lights. For those who are staying in remote locations or aurora lodges, this process becomes easier—simply step outside, look up, and be ready to wait.

If you're traveling specifically to see the auroras, it's important to plan for several nights of viewing. The northern lights are unpredictable, and it's entirely possible to have a stretch of cloudy or quiet nights. Giving yourself multiple opportunities to see the lights increases your odds of catching them at their peak.

One of the most common questions asked by aurora watchers is, "How long do the northern lights last?" The answer, like so much with the aurora borealis, varies. Auroras can flicker into existence for just a few minutes, or they can stay in the sky for hours at a time, shifting and pulsing in waves.

When the northern lights first appear, they often start as faint green glimmers on the horizon, slowly growing brighter and more intense. In some cases, the display will last just a few minutes before fading back into darkness. In other cases, the lights will build into a dramatic crescendo of color and movement, lasting for several hours before dissipating.

The key to experiencing the full beauty of the auroras is patience. Even if the lights appear faint or distant at first, it's worth staying outside and watching for a while. Aurora displays often evolve and change over time, with periods of intense activity followed by quieter moments. Don't be surprised if the lights disappear for a few minutes, only to return in a different part of the sky, brighter and more vivid than before.

The Role of Geomagnetic Activity

As we've discussed in earlier chapters, the strength of the northern lights is closely tied to geomagnetic activity. During periods of low activity, the auroras may be faint and restricted to the far north. But when a geomagnetic storm hits, the lights can explode into life, stretching far beyond the polar regions and lighting up the skies in vibrant colors.

The intensity of the northern lights is directly related to the KP index, which measures geomagnetic activity on a scale from 0 to 9. A KP index of 3 or 4 means that auroras are likely to be visible in northern latitudes, but the display may be relatively weak. A KP index of 5 or higher indicates a geomagnetic storm, which can lead to more intense auroral displays and greater visibility in lower latitudes.

During periods of high geomagnetic activity, the auroras often last longer and cover a larger portion of the sky. This is when you're most likely to see those dramatic, swirling curtains of light that fill the horizon. For serious aurora chasers, keeping an eye on the KP index and solar activity is essential for predicting when the lights will be at their best.

While there's no surefire way to guarantee you'll see the northern lights, there are a few strategies that can help improve your chances.

1. **Stay Up Late and Be Patient**: The northern lights often appear late at night, so be prepared to stay up and wait for them. Bring warm clothing, blankets, and snacks if you're heading out for a long night of aurora watching. Patience is key—sometimes the lights don't appear until well after midnight, but the wait is always worth it.

2. **Get Away from Light Pollution**: To see the northern lights in all their glory, you'll need to get away from city lights and other sources of light pollution. Rural areas, national parks, and remote wilderness lodges offer the

best viewing conditions. Even in aurora hotspots like Fairbanks, Alaska, or Tromsø, Norway, it's worth venturing a little farther out to find darker skies.

3. **Check the Weather and KP Index**: Cloud cover can ruin an otherwise perfect night of aurora watching, so always check the weather forecast before heading out. Clear skies are essential for seeing the lights. Additionally, monitoring the KP index and geomagnetic forecasts can give you a good sense of when the auroras are likely to be most active.

4. **Give Yourself Multiple Chances**: If you're traveling to see the northern lights, plan to stay for several nights. The lights don't appear on command, and it's possible to have stretches of cloudy or quiet nights. By giving yourself multiple opportunities to see the auroras, you increase your chances of catching a display.

5. **Keep an Open Mind**: Finally, remember that the northern lights are a natural phenomenon, and they don't follow a set schedule. Sometimes the most breathtaking auroras appear when you least expect them. Stay flexible and be ready to embrace the moment when the sky comes alive.

In many ways, chasing the northern lights feels like time travel. You stand beneath the vast, starry sky, waiting for a glimpse of something timeless and cosmic. The auroras connect us to the rhythms of the sun, the Earth, and the universe beyond. Whether you're watching the lights flicker on the horizon or witnessing a full-blown geomagnetic storm, there's a sense that you're part of something bigger—an ancient dance of light and energy that's been playing out for millennia.

For those who are patient and persistent, the northern lights offer a reward like no other. When the sky finally lights up, and the colors start to swirl above you, it feels like a gift from the universe, a reminder of the beauty and mystery that still surrounds us.

In the next chapter, we'll dive into the art of capturing the northern lights through photography—because once you've seen them with your own eyes, you'll want to bring a piece of that magic home with you.

Chapter 6: Photography of the Northern Lights

Watching the northern lights swirl and pulse across the night sky is an experience you'll never forget. The colors, the movement, the sheer magic of it all can leave you breathless. But once you've had the privilege of seeing this extraordinary spectacle, the next step is often trying to capture it—freezing that fleeting moment in time so you can relive it later and share it with others. Photographing the aurora borealis, however, is no easy feat. The lights don't follow a set schedule, and they certainly don't wait for you to set up your camera. It takes preparation, patience, and a bit of technical know-how to get the perfect shot.

This chapter will guide you through the basics of photographing the northern lights, from camera settings to gear to finding the perfect spot. We'll also explore the stories behind some of the world's most iconic aurora photos and what it takes to capture the magic of the lights in a single frame.

When it comes to photographing the northern lights, patience is your most valuable tool. Unlike a traditional landscape shot, where the scene is static, the auroras are constantly changing. They flicker and fade, grow brighter, then disappear entirely, only to return minutes or hours later in a completely different form. It's a moving target, and as a photographer, you have to be ready to capture the lights at their best.

Before you even start thinking about camera settings or composition, the first step is preparing yourself for the conditions. If you're heading into the wilderness to photograph the northern lights, you'll need to be dressed warmly and ready to stay outside for hours at a time. Aurora photography often means standing in freezing temperatures, sometimes in the middle of the night, waiting for the lights to appear. It's essential to be comfortable so you can focus on your photography and not just on staying warm.

Here are a few key things to remember before you head out to shoot the auroras:

1. **Dress in Layers**: You'll be outside for an extended period, likely in subzero temperatures. Wear layers of clothing, including thermal underwear, wool socks, insulated boots, and a good down jacket. Don't forget gloves that allow you to manipulate your camera controls without exposing your fingers to the cold.

2. **Bring Snacks and Hot Drinks**: Waiting for the northern lights can take time, and it's important to stay warm and energized. Pack some snacks and a thermos of hot coffee, tea, or cocoa to keep you comfortable during the long hours outside.

3. **Bring Extra Camera Batteries**: Cold temperatures can drain your camera batteries faster than usual, so it's a good idea to bring extras. Keep spare batteries in an inner pocket close to your body to keep them warm and ready for use.

Once you're prepared for the conditions, it's time to turn your attention to your camera and settings.

The Right Gear for Aurora Photography

You don't need the most expensive camera on the market to take great photos of the northern lights, but there are a few essential pieces of gear that will make your life much easier. Here's what you'll need:

1. **A DSLR or Mirrorless Camera**: While you can take aurora photos with a smartphone or point-and-shoot camera, a DSLR or mirrorless camera will give you the most control over settings like shutter speed, ISO, and aperture. These features are essential for capturing the northern lights, which require long exposures to bring out their full color and detail.

2. **A Wide-Angle Lens**: A wide-angle lens (something in the 14mm to 24mm range) is ideal for aurora photography because it allows you to capture more of the sky in a single frame. Look for a lens with a fast aperture (f/2.8 or lower) to let in as much light as possible.

3. **A Sturdy Tripod**: Long-exposure photography requires the camera to be completely still, so a tripod is a must. Make sure it's sturdy enough to withstand wind or uneven ground, as you'll often be shooting in rough conditions.

4. **A Remote Shutter Release**: To avoid shaking the camera when pressing the shutter button, use a remote shutter release or set your camera's timer to a few seconds.

Camera Settings for Photography

The key to photographing the northern lights is understanding how to balance your camera settings to capture as much light as possible while keeping the auroras crisp and in focus. Here's a basic starting point for your settings:

1. **Shutter Speed**: Start with a shutter speed of about **5 to 15 seconds**. This will give the camera enough time to capture the movement of the auroras without making them too blurry. If the lights are particularly fast-moving, you may need to use a shorter shutter speed (around 3 to 5 seconds) to keep them sharp.

2. **Aperture**: Set your lens aperture to its widest setting (usually **f/2.8** or lower) to allow as much light as possible to enter the camera. The northern lights are bright, but the surrounding landscape is often dark, so you want to maximize the light your camera is capturing.

3. **ISO**: Start with an ISO setting of around **800 to 1600**. If the auroras are bright, you can lower the ISO to reduce noise. If they're faint, you may need to raise the ISO to get more light into your shot, but be careful not to go too high, as this can introduce grain into your images.

4. **Focus**: Manually focus your lens to infinity to ensure that the stars and auroras are sharp. Auto-focus doesn't work well in low-light conditions, so it's best to set your focus manually before you start shooting.

5. **White Balance**: Set your white balance to "daylight" or "auto" to capture the natural colors of the auroras. You can always adjust the white balance later in post-processing, but starting with a neutral setting helps preserve the true colors.

Making the Most of the Landscape

Photographing the northern lights is about more than just capturing the auroras themselves—it's about composing an image that tells a story. The sky may be the star of the show, but the landscape around you can add depth and context to the scene.

1. **Foreground Interest**: Including elements of the landscape in your shot can create a more dynamic image. Whether it's a silhouette of trees, a mountain range, or a frozen lake reflecting the lights, adding a foreground element gives your photo scale and helps the viewer connect with the scene.

2. **Leading Lines**: Look for natural features in the landscape that can guide the viewer's eye toward the auroras. This could be a road, a river, or the curve of a hill. These leading lines draw attention to the northern lights and add a sense of movement to the image.

3. **Capture the Movement**: The auroras are constantly shifting, which can create beautiful patterns and shapes in the sky. Experiment with different shutter speeds to capture the unique movement of the lights. A shorter exposure will freeze the auroras in place, while a longer exposure will create a smoother, more flowing effect.

4. **Be Flexible**: The northern lights are unpredictable, so be ready to adapt your composition as they move across the sky. Sometimes the best shot isn't the one you planned—it's the one you catch on the fly as the lights shift in unexpected ways.

Enhancing Your Aurora Photos

After a night of shooting the northern lights, you'll likely have dozens (or hundreds) of photos to sort through. Post-processing is an important part of bringing out the best in your aurora shots. Here are a few tips for editing your photos:

1. **Adjust Exposure**: Depending on the brightness of the auroras and the surrounding landscape, you may need to tweak the exposure to balance the image. Be careful not to overexpose the auroras themselves, as this can wash out their colors.

2. **Enhance Colors**: The colors of the northern lights are naturally vivid, but a bit of post-processing can help bring out the greens, purples, and reds. Use your editing software to gently increase saturation and vibrance but avoid overdoing it—your goal is to enhance the natural beauty of the lights, not create an unrealistic image.

3. **Reduce Noise**: If you were shooting with a high ISO, you might notice some noise in your images, especially in the darker areas. Use noise reduction tools to clean up the image without sacrificing too much detail.

4. **Crop for Composition**: Sometimes the best way to improve an aurora photo is to crop the image. If the lights were concentrated in one part of the sky, cropping out unnecessary foreground or empty space can create a more impactful composition.

Iconic Aurora Photos

Some of the world's most iconic photos of the northern lights are the result of years of experience, planning, and a bit of luck. Behind every great aurora photo is a story—of cold nights spent waiting, of last-minute decisions to drive to a new location, or of perfect timing as the lights burst into life.

One famous photo that captivated the world was taken in Abisko, Sweden, where the auroras reflected perfectly off the frozen Torneträsk Lake. The photographer had been waiting for several hours in the cold when the lights appeared, creating an otherworldly scene that seemed almost too beautiful to be real.

In Iceland, a photographer captured the northern lights dancing over the iconic Kirkjufell mountain. The auroras framed the peak perfectly, casting a green glow over the landscape. This photo quickly became one of the most famous images of the northern lights, shared across social media and used in countless travel promotions for Iceland.

These stories remind us that while photographing the northern lights takes skill and preparation, it's also about being in the right place at the right time. Nature doesn't always cooperate, but when it does, the results can be breathtaking.

For many photographers, capturing the northern lights becomes an obsession. Once you've seen the lights and successfully photographed them, you'll likely find yourself wanting to do it again and again. The good news is that no two aurora displays are ever the same, so there's always something new to discover and capture. Whether you're a seasoned photographer or just starting out, photographing the northern lights is an experience like no other. It's a chance to connect with the natural world in a profound way, to witness something truly awe-inspiring, and to bring a piece of that magic home with you. So grab your camera, bundle up, and get ready for the adventure of a lifetime— because the northern lights are waiting.

Chapter 7: The Myths and Mysteries

For thousands of years, humans have looked up at the sky in wonder as the northern lights flickered and danced across the heavens. Long before science offered explanations, ancient civilizations created their own stories about what these mysterious lights meant. To them, the auroras weren't just a natural phenomenon—they were messages from the gods, spirits, or omens of events yet to come. Even now, after we understand the science behind the aurora borealis, the myths and mysteries that surround the northern lights still capture our imaginations.

In this chapter, we'll dive into some of the most fascinating legends from cultures around the world, explore the lingering mysteries that science hasn't yet fully explained, and reflect on how the auroras continue to inspire awe and reverence.

The northern lights have inspired countless stories across the globe, each reflecting the beliefs and traditions of the culture that created them. From the Vikings of Scandinavia to the Inuit of the Arctic, different peoples have looked to the sky and seen the lights as symbols of something far greater than themselves. Here are a few of the most enduring myths surrounding the auroras.

The Norse Valkyries: Warriors of the Sky

In Norse mythology, the auroras were often associated with the Valkyries—legendary female warriors who chose which soldiers would live and die in battle. The Norse believed that the northern lights were the reflections of the Valkyries' armor as they rode through the sky on horseback, guiding the souls of fallen warriors to Valhalla, the afterlife for the bravest fighters.

The imagery of shining, armored women racing through the heavens was a fitting explanation for the ethereal beauty of the auroras. To the Norse, the lights were a reminder of their warrior culture and the honor of dying in battle. When the sky lit up with the northern lights, it was seen as a sign that the gods were watching over them and that the bravest warriors were being taken to their eternal rest.

The Inuit: Spirits Playing in the Sky

For the Inuit people of the Arctic, the northern lights were deeply spiritual, often believed to be the souls of ancestors playing in the sky. Some Inuit stories describe the auroras as spirits playing a game similar to football, tossing a walrus skull back and forth in the night sky. The movement of the lights was thought to be the spirits dancing and celebrating in the afterlife.

Other Inuit tribes believed the auroras could be a bridge between the physical world and the spiritual world. Shamans were thought to have the ability to communicate with the lights, using their flickering patterns as messages from the ancestors or the gods. This belief gave the auroras a mystical quality, turning them into something to be revered rather than feared.

The Finnish Fox: Fire in the Sky

In Finland, one of the most charming myths about the northern lights involves a magical arctic fox. According to Finnish legend, the northern lights are created by this fox as it runs across the snowy landscape, sweeping its bushy tail across the ground. As the fox runs, it kicks up snowflakes that are transformed into sparks of light, which shoot up into the sky, creating the auroras.

This story not only explains the lights but also ties them to the natural world, reflecting the deep connection the Finnish people have with their snowy, wintry environment. The Finnish word for the northern lights, "revontulet," literally translates to "fox fires," honoring this enchanting myth.

Indigenous North America: Spirits and Warnings

Many Indigenous tribes in North America had their own interpretations of the northern lights. For some, the auroras were seen as the spirits of ancestors or animals that had passed on. The Cree believed the lights were the souls of the dead, while the Algonquin tribe believed they were the spirits of hunters lighting fires in the northern sky to guide them.

In other tribes, the northern lights were seen as omens of danger or warning. The Kwakiutl of the Pacific Northwest believed that the auroras were a sign of impending conflict or natural disaster, while the Menominee people believed that the lights were torches held by giant spirits who were gathering to hunt sturgeon at night. These interpretations gave the auroras a more ominous tone, associating them with the unknown forces that governed life and death.

A Sign of Fertility and Good Fortune

In Japan, the northern lights are thought to bring good luck and are sometimes considered a sign of fertility. Couples who conceive a child under the northern lights are believed to be blessed with good fortune and happiness. This tradition has made aurora-viewing a popular activity for couples, particularly those hoping to start a family.

The romantic notion of the northern lights as a bringer of love and prosperity contrasts with some of the more ominous legends of other cultures. It's a reminder that the auroras, like all natural phenomena, are open to interpretation, with their beauty inspiring different feelings in different people.

While modern science has uncovered most of the secrets behind the northern lights, there are still a few mysteries that continue to puzzle researchers. These lingering questions add to the aura of mystery that surrounds the auroras, keeping alive the sense that we don't fully understand everything about the universe just yet.

One of the most intriguing mysteries is whether the northern lights make sounds. For centuries, people have reported hearing faint crackling, hissing, or rustling noises when the auroras are particularly bright and close. These sounds are often described as similar to the sound of static or the faint rustle of leaves in the wind.

Despite these reports, scientists have had difficulty proving that the auroras produce audible sounds. The lights themselves occur so high in the atmosphere—often over 60 miles above the Earth—that it seems unlikely any sound could travel that far. However, recent research suggests that it might be possible for the auroras to produce low-frequency electromagnetic waves that could generate sound close to the ground.

The debate over whether the northern lights can be heard remains ongoing, adding a layer of mystery to the experience of aurora-watching. Could it be that ancient stories of spirits whispering in the sky were inspired by these faint, elusive sounds?

Most of us associate the northern lights with shades of green, purple, and blue, but under certain conditions, the auroras can appear red. These red auroras are much rarer and often more subdued than their green counterparts, making them a highly sought-after sight for aurora chasers.

The science behind the red auroras is still being studied. While we know that the color is caused by particles colliding with oxygen at higher altitudes, the precise conditions that produce this phenomenon are less well understood. Red auroras tend to appear during periods of intense solar activity, but they can also be faint and difficult to spot, making them an elusive part of the auroral display.

For those lucky enough to witness a red aurora, the sight is unforgettable. The deep crimson hue seems to fill the sky with an otherworldly glow, creating a scene that feels both beautiful and slightly eerie.

While the northern lights, or aurora borealis, are well-known and well-documented, their southern counterpart—the aurora australis—remains shrouded in mystery. The aurora australis occurs in the southern hemisphere and is visible from places like Antarctica, southern New Zealand, and the southern tip of South America. However, because these regions are far less populated than the northern latitudes, sightings of the southern lights are much rarer.

The aurora australis behaves similarly to the northern lights, but scientists still have questions about whether the two phenomena are perfectly symmetrical. Since fewer people have witnessed the southern lights, our understanding of them is still somewhat limited, adding to the sense of mystery that surrounds this lesser-known aurora.

Even in a world where we can explain much of what we see in the sky, the northern lights retain their sense of wonder and magic. Whether you view them as a natural phenomenon, a spiritual experience, or a cosmic mystery, the auroras continue to inspire awe in everyone who has the privilege of seeing them.

The myths and legends that have grown around the northern lights reflect humanity's deep connection to the natural world. In every culture, the auroras have been seen as something extraordinary—something that connects us to the heavens, to our ancestors, and to the mysteries of the universe.

Perhaps that's why the northern lights continue to captivate us, even in the age of science. For all the technology and understanding we've gained, there's still something about the lights that feels magical. They remind us that we are just a small part of a much larger, more complex universe, and that sometimes, the most beautiful things are the ones we can't fully explain.

Chapter 8: The Future of Auroras

The aurora borealis has danced across the skies for millions of years, its lights witnessed by ancient civilizations, explorers, and now, modern-day travelers. Yet, as we stand in awe beneath its shimmering colors, a question lingers in the back of our minds: Will these lights always be here? The thought of the northern lights disappearing seems impossible, yet climate change, solar cycles, and changes in our atmosphere might one day affect how often and how intensely we see this celestial display.

In this chapter, we'll explore the potential future of the northern lights, what factors could influence their visibility in the years to come, and how changing global conditions might affect this ancient natural wonder. We'll also look at the solar cycles that govern auroral activity and consider whether future generations will be as lucky as we are to witness this incredible phenomenon.

A Cosmic Rhythm

To understand the future of the northern lights, we first need to look at the source of their power: the sun. The northern lights are driven by solar activity—specifically, the solar wind and charged particles that stream from the sun and interact with Earth's magnetic field. This activity doesn't happen randomly; instead, it follows a predictable pattern known as the solar cycle.

The solar cycle lasts approximately 11 years, during which the sun's activity increases and decreases in a regular rhythm. At the peak of the cycle, known as the solar maximum, the sun is most active, producing more solar flares and coronal mass ejections (CMEs) that lead to increased geomagnetic storms on Earth. This is when auroral activity is at its highest, and the lights can be seen more frequently and in more places.

During the solar minimum, which marks the low point of the cycle, the sun is quieter, producing fewer solar storms and, consequently, fewer auroras. The northern lights still occur during the solar minimum, but they are less intense and tend to be visible only in the far northern latitudes.

We are currently moving toward the next solar maximum, expected to occur around 2025. This means that in the coming years, auroral displays should become more frequent and intense, providing a golden opportunity for skywatchers and aurora chasers.

However, what happens beyond this cycle? What will the northern lights look like as we continue to experience the natural fluctuations of the solar cycle—and how might human activity play a role in their future?

Climate Change and the Northern Lights

While the northern lights are primarily influenced by solar activity, Earth's changing climate may also play a role in how we experience auroras in the future. Climate change is altering weather patterns, shifting seasons, and increasing temperatures across the globe, and these changes may indirectly affect aurora visibility.

One of the most significant factors is the potential increase in cloud cover. For aurora watchers, clear skies are essential to seeing the lights, and a rise in average global temperatures could lead to more frequent cloudiness in traditionally clear regions. Areas like Alaska, northern Canada, and Scandinavia, which have long been considered aurora hotspots, may see more frequent overcast conditions during the winter months, making it harder to catch a glimpse of the northern lights.

Additionally, climate change is causing the Arctic to warm faster than any other region on Earth. This warming could alter weather patterns in the far north, potentially affecting the pristine conditions that make places like Tromsø or Fairbanks ideal for aurora viewing. While the northern lights themselves won't be directly impacted by climate change, the ability to see them may become more challenging in the years to come if cloud cover increases or weather becomes more unpredictable.

The Ionosphere and Human Activity

Another area of concern is how human activity might affect the ionosphere, the layer of Earth's atmosphere where the northern lights occur. The ionosphere is home to charged particles that interact with solar wind to create the auroras, but it is also increasingly being affected by human-made technologies, such as satellites, radio communications, and even space tourism.

There is a growing body of research that suggests human activity could influence the behavior of the ionosphere in subtle ways. For example, high-frequency radio waves used for communication can alter the ionosphere's composition, potentially affecting the way auroras form or how they are perceived from the ground. While these changes are unlikely to make the auroras disappear, they could lead to slight variations in the way the lights behave.

In addition, the rise of **space tourism** cou.d introduce new challenges for aurora viewing. With more satellites and spaceflights taking place in the upper atmosphere, there is a chance that light pollution from human-made objects could interfere with the northern lights, especially if space tourism becomes more widespread in the coming decades. Imagine standing in the wilderness, ready to capture the auroras, only to have the display interrupted by a satellite streaking across the sky or artificial lights from space stations.

Could the Northern Lights Disappear?

The idea of the northern lights disappearing entirely seems far-fetched, but it's not impossible. The northern lights rely on Earth's magnetic field to guide solar particles toward the poles, where they interact with our atmosphere to create the auroras. If, for any reason, Earth's magnetic field were to weaken or change dramatically, it could alter the way auroras form—or even prevent them from occurring at all.

One of the potential causes of concern is the **shifting of Earth's magnetic poles**. The magnetic north pole is not fixed—it drifts slowly over time, and recent data suggests that it has been moving more rapidly in recent years. While this drift is not expected to have immediate effects on the northern lights, a dramatic shift in the magnetic field (or even a **magnetic pole reversal,** where the poles swap places) could impact auroral activity in ways that are still not fully understood.

A pole reversal is a rare event that has happened several times in Earth's history, most recently about **780,000 years ago**. If it were to happen again, it's possible that the locations of the auroras would change, and the northern lights as we know them could be seen in entirely different parts of the world. However, this is a long-term possibility, and scientists are still studying the effects of such a reversal on the Earth's magnetic field.

For now, the northern lights are safe—but the long-term future remains an open question, and ongoing research will be key to understanding what lies ahead.

The Future of Aurora Chasing

While the northern lights are not disappearing anytime soon, there's no denying that aurora chasing will evolve in the coming years. With climate change, technological advancements, and the natural fluctuations of the solar cycle, the experience of viewing the northern lights may change for future generations.

One positive aspect of the future is the role of technology in making aurora chasing more accessible. As apps, forecasts, and real-time tracking become even more advanced, more people will have the opportunity to plan their trips and chase the lights with greater precision. Drones and new camera technology will allow photographers to capture the auroras in ways that were once unimaginable, bringing the beauty of the northern lights to people around the world, even if they can't witness it in person.

At the same time, the global movement toward **sustainable travel** may help preserve the pristine environments that make aurora viewing so special. As travelers become more conscious of their environmental impact, there is hope that the wilderness areas where the northern lights are most visible will be protected and preserved for future generations.

The northern lights have been a part of Earth's story for millions of years, and they continue to inspire and captivate people from all walks of life. As we look toward the future, it's clear that the auroras will remain a powerful symbol of the beauty and mystery of our planet.

Whether we're standing beneath the Arctic sky, marveling at the lights in their full glory, or using technology to predict the next big solar storm, the northern lights connect us to something greater than ourselves. They remind us that we are part of a living, breathing planet, one that is constantly evolving and changing, yet always full of wonder.

The future may bring new challenges and changes, but the magic of the northern lights will endure. For as long as the sun continues to send its energy our way, and as long as Earth's magnetic field remains, the auroras will dance across the sky—perhaps in new forms, perhaps in new places—but always as a reminder of the beauty and power of the natural world.

Chapter 9: Common Misconceptions

The northern lights are one of the most mysterious and magical natural phenomena on Earth, and as with anything so awe-inspiring, they come with plenty of questions. People around the world are fascinated by the aurora borealis, but they often have misunderstandings about how it works, when they can see it, or even why it happens. In this chapter, we'll address some of the most frequently asked questions about the northern lights and clear up common misconceptions.

Whether you're planning your first trip to see the auroras or you've been chasing the lights for years, this guide will help you understand more about the science behind the lights, the best ways to see them, and what to expect when you finally catch a glimpse of nature's most spectacular light show.

How Long Do the Northern Lights Last?

One of the most common questions is how long a northern lights display typically lasts. The truth is, it varies depending on the strength of the geomagnetic activity and local weather conditions. An aurora display can last anywhere from a few minutes to several hours.

In some cases, you might see the lights flicker in the sky for just a brief moment before disappearing. This happens when the geomagnetic activity is weak or the conditions aren't perfect. However, during stronger geomagnetic storms, the auroras can remain visible for hours, with the intensity of the lights waxing and waning throughout the night.

Aurora displays often come in waves, so even if the lights seem to fade, it's worth waiting to see if they return. Sometimes the best part of the show happens after a lull in activity. If the KP index is high and the sky is clear, you could be treated to a spectacular display that lasts all night long.

Can I See the Northern Lights from Anywhere?

While the northern lights are more common in certain regions of the world, under the right conditions, they can be seen from places far outside the typical auroral zones. The auroras are most often visible in high-latitude regions near the Arctic Circle, including Norway, Sweden, Finland, Iceland, Alaska, northern Canada, and Russia.

However, during periods of intense solar activity, the northern lights can stretch much further south. For example, during strong geomagnetic storms, the auroras have been visible in parts of the United States, including Ohio, New York, and even Texas. In Europe, the lights have occasionally been spotted as far south as France and Spain.

That said, your chances of seeing the northern lights increase the closer you are to the poles. If you're hoping to catch a glimpse of the auroras, it's best to head to a high-latitude location with clear, dark skies.

Why Can't I See the Northern Lights Right Now?

Many people assume that the northern lights should be visible whenever they travel to places known for aurora activity, but the truth is, the lights are highly unpredictable. Even in aurora hotspots like Tromsø, Norway, or Fairbanks, Alaska, it's possible to spend several nights without seeing the lights due to cloud cover, low solar activity, or other factors.

There are a few common reasons why you might not be seeing the auroras:

1. **Cloud Cover**: Even if geomagnetic activity is high, you won't see the northern lights if the sky is covered in clouds. Always check the weather forecast before heading out to view the auroras, and try to find a location with clear skies.

2. **Solar Activity**: The northern lights are driven by solar activity, so if the sun isn't producing enough solar wind, the lights won't appear. Checking the KP index can give you a sense of whether the conditions are right for auroral activity. A KP index of **5** or higher is ideal for strong displays.

3. **Light Pollution**: If you're in or near a city, the artificial lights can wash out the northern lights, making them difficult to see. For the best aurora experience, head to a remote area with minimal light pollution.

What Colors Can the Northern Lights Be?

Most people associate the northern lights with shades of green, but the auroras can actually appear in a variety of colors, depending on the type of gas particles they interact with and the altitude at which the collisions occur.

- **Green**: The most common color, green auroras are caused by oxygen atoms at lower altitudes (around 60 miles above Earth). This is the color most people think of when they imagine the northern lights.

- **Red**: Less common but incredibly striking, red auroras occur when solar particles collide with oxygen atoms at much higher altitudes (above 150 miles). These red auroras are often faint and may only appear at the edges of a green auroral display.

- **Purple and Blue**: Auroras can also appear in shades of purple or blue, which are caused by the interaction of solar particles with nitrogen in the atmosphere. These colors are typically seen at the lower edges of an auroral display and are more visible during periods of strong geomagnetic activity.

While green auroras are the most frequent, it's worth keeping an eye out for these rarer colors. During particularly intense displays, the northern lights can take on a full spectrum of hues, creating a breathtaking and multicolored sky.

Do the Northern Lights Make a Sound?

For centuries, people who have witnessed the northern lights have reported hearing strange sounds, like crackling or faint hissing, accompanying the light show. While these reports have long been considered anecdotal, some scientific studies suggest that the northern lights might indeed produce sounds under certain conditions.

The theory is that the auroras may cause electromagnetic disturbances that produce sounds at ground level, particularly in very quiet environments. These sounds are extremely faint and difficult to detect, which is why they aren't commonly heard.

However, most aurora watchers will experience the lights in silence. Whether or not the northern lights make noise remains one of the enduring mysteries of this natural phenomenon.

Can the Northern Lights Harm Us?

Although the northern lights are produced by charged particles from the sun interacting with Earth's atmosphere, they pose no direct danger to people on the ground. The particles that create the auroras are guided by Earth's magnetic field and occur far above the surface, usually around 60 to 300 miles in altitude.

That said, the geomagnetic storms that produce the northern lights can sometimes interfere with electronic systems, including GPS signals, power grids, and satellite communications. During periods of intense solar activity, scientists monitor geomagnetic storms to ensure that any potential disruptions to technology are minimized.

For aurora chasers on the ground, though, the northern lights are completely safe to watch and enjoy.

Are the Northern Lights the Same as the Southern Lights?

Yes, the northern lights (aurora borealis) and the southern lights (aurora australis) are essentially the same phenomenon, occurring in opposite hemispheres. Both are caused by solar wind interacting with Earth's magnetic field, and they produce similar light displays in the polar regions.

The main difference between the two is location. The aurora australis is visible in the southern hemisphere, particularly from Antarctica, southern New Zealand, and parts of Tasmania and Argentina. Because these regions are less populated and harder to access than the northern hemisphere's auroral hotspots, the southern lights are less frequently observed and documented.

However, for those adventurous enough to travel to the southern latitudes, the aurora australis offers the same breathtaking beauty as its northern counterpart.

Is There a Best Month to See the Northern Lights?

The best months to see the northern lights depend on where you're located, but generally, the optimal time for aurora viewing is between September and March. During these months, the nights are long and dark, providing the best conditions for aurora visibility.

In the far north, places like Alaska, Iceland, and Norway experience long, dark winters, making the northern lights visible throughout the night. The months of December through February often have the clearest skies, but September, October, and March are also excellent times for viewing, especially as they tend to have milder weather.

Keep in mind that the northern lights are not visible during the summer months in the Arctic because the sun doesn't set for long enough to create the darkness required for aurora viewing.

How Far in Advance Can the Northern Lights Be Predicted?

While scientists can track solar activity and predict periods of heightened geomagnetic activity, predicting the northern lights with absolute accuracy is challenging. Typically, short-term aurora forecasts can give you a 1 to 3-day window of when the lights are likely to be visible based on solar activity and the KP index.

For more precise forecasts, aurora trackers and apps can provide real-time data about geomagnetic storms and solar winds. These tools allow you to monitor the likelihood of auroras on a nightly basis, giving you the best chance to plan your viewing experience.

Can You See the Northern Lights from a Plane?

Yes, under the right conditions, it is possible to see the northern lights from a plane. Flights that pass over polar regions or northern latitudes (such as transatlantic flights between Europe and North America) often provide a unique opportunity to witness the auroras from above the clouds.

If you're flying at night and the auroral activity is strong, keep an eye on the northern horizon, and you might catch a glimpse of the lights from the window of your plane. Some airlines even offer special aurora viewing flights, where the entire journey is dedicated to chasing the northern lights.

Chapter 10: The Call of the Northern Lights

Standing beneath the northern lights is an experience that transcends words. No matter how many photos you've seen or stories you've heard, nothing prepares you for the moment when the sky explodes into light, and you're suddenly standing beneath a living, breathing canvas of color. The lights seem to move in response to some unseen rhythm, weaving across the sky like ethereal dancers. For many, witnessing the northern lights isn't just a bucket-list item—it's a transformative experience, one that stays with you long after the lights have faded from the horizon.

In this final chapter, we reflect on what it means to chase the northern lights. Beyond the science, the logistics, and the practical tips, what draws people back time and again to stand in the cold, hoping for just one more glimpse of the auroras? What is it about the lights that speaks so deeply to us? And how can we ensure that this experience remains available to future generations?

Let's embark on one last journey together, to explore the deeper meaning behind the northern lights and the enduring allure of this natural wonder.

The Personal Pilgrimage: Why We Chase the Lights

Chasing the northern lights is about more than simply seeing a spectacle. For many, it becomes a personal pilgrimage, a way of connecting with something larger than ourselves. People travel from all corners of the globe to witness the auroras, and while their motivations may vary, there's a shared sense of wonder and reverence that unites aurora chasers.

One of the most striking things about the northern lights is their fleeting, unpredictable nature. Unlike other natural wonders that are fixed in place—majestic mountains or grand waterfalls—the auroras are elusive. You can't schedule a viewing or guarantee that you'll see them, no matter how much planning you do. The northern lights follow their own rules, appearing when the conditions are right, then vanishing just as quickly. This unpredictability adds to the thrill of the chase.

For many, chasing the lights becomes a quest, a test of patience and persistence. It requires a willingness to endure cold nights, long waits, and sometimes disappointment. But when the lights do appear, that moment is all the more magical because you've worked for it, because you've stood in the dark and waited, unsure if you'd be rewarded. In a world where so much is certain and controlled, the northern lights remind us that some things are still wild, mysterious, and beyond our control.

The Global Community of Aurora Chasers

Over the years, a global community of aurora enthusiasts has grown around the shared experience of chasing the northern lights. Social media, apps, and websites have brought together people from all walks of life who share a common passion for the auroras. Whether they're seasoned photographers, first-time travelers, or locals who live beneath the auroral oval, these people are united by their love for the lights.

Online forums and groups dedicated to aurora hunting have become spaces for sharing tips, stories, and photos. People post updates about where the lights are most visible, offer advice on the best camera settings, and even organize meet-ups to chase the auroras together. For many, being part of this community adds a social dimension to what is often a solitary pursuit. Chasing the northern lights is no longer just an individual experience—it's a shared journey, connecting people across borders and continents.

Beyond the online world, some dedicated aurora chasers travel the globe in search of the perfect display. These are the people who plan their vacations around solar activity, who know the KP index as well as they know their own address, and who will fly across the world at a moment's notice if there's a chance to see a particularly strong geomagnetic storm. For them, chasing the northern lights isn't just a hobby—it's a way of life.

Finding Meaning in the Lights

Why do the northern lights resonate so deeply with people? There's no single answer, but for many, the auroras are a reminder of the beauty and mystery that still exists in our world. In an age where we've mapped every corner of the Earth and can access almost any information with the touch of a button, the northern lights remain unpredictable and untouchable. They remind us that there are forces at play in the universe that we still don't fully understand.

Standing beneath the northern lights, many people describe a feeling of humility. The auroras are a reminder of how small we are in the grand scheme of things, how vast and powerful the natural world truly is. For a moment, we're pulled out of our everyday lives and into something timeless and cosmic. The lights connect us to the rhythms of the universe—the solar wind, the Earth's magnetic field, the dance of particles high above our atmosphere. They show us that we are part of a larger story, one that has been unfolding for millions of years.

For some, the northern lights also carry a spiritual significance. In many cultures, the auroras are seen as messages from the gods, spirits, or ancestors. Even today, people who witness the lights often describe the experience as spiritual, as if they've been granted a glimpse of something divine. The lights are a reminder that there is more to the world than what we can see or explain.

Protecting the Future of Aurora Chasing

As we look to the future, it's important to recognize that the experience of chasing the northern lights isn't guaranteed. Climate change, light pollution, and other human activities could affect the ability of future generations to witness the auroras in their full glory. As more people travel to see the lights, there's also a need to ensure that this tourism is sustainable and doesn't harm the fragile environments where the lights are most visible.

One of the most immediate threats to aurora viewing is light pollution. As cities grow and artificial lights spread, it becomes harder to find dark skies where the auroras can be seen clearly. Even in remote areas, the glow from nearby towns or industrial sites can interfere with the visibility of the lights. Efforts to reduce light pollution—through dark sky reserves, responsible lighting practices, and public awareness campaigns—are essential if we want to preserve the ability to see the northern lights in the future.

Additionally, as climate change alters weather patterns, it may become more difficult to predict the ideal conditions for aurora viewing. Warmer temperatures could lead to increased cloud cover in some regions, making it harder to find clear skies for viewing. Protecting the natural environments where the northern lights are most visible—such as the Arctic wilderness—will be crucial in preserving the aurora experience for future generations.

Carrying the Light Forward

Despite the challenges, there is hope that the northern lights will continue to inspire and captivate people for generations to come. As long as the sun continues to send its energy toward Earth, and as long as our planet's magnetic field remains strong, the auroras will dance across the sky, just as they have for millions of years.

For those who have experienced the northern lights, the memory stays with them, a glowing reminder of the beauty and mystery that exists in the world. For those still waiting for their first glimpse, the call of the lights is always there—a promise of adventure, wonder, and awe.

In the end, the northern lights are more than just a natural phenomenon. They are a symbol of our connection to the universe, of the beauty that exists beyond our understanding, and of the enduring mystery that keeps us looking up at the night sky in wonder. Whether you're standing in the Arctic wilderness or watching from your backyard during a rare southern display, the northern lights are a reminder that there is magic in the world, waiting to be discovered.

So, as you chase the lights—whether for the first time or the hundredth—carry that sense of wonder with you. The auroras may be fleeting, but the memory of their beauty lasts a lifetime.

Chapter 11: Journey Through Art and Culture

The northern lights have not only captured the attention of scientists and travelers—they have also left a deep imprint on the arts, inspiring countless works of literature, painting, music, and film. From ancient myths passed down through generations to modern interpretations in visual and performing arts, the auroras are a powerful symbol of mystery, beauty, and transformation.

In this chapter, we will explore how the aurora borealis has influenced artistic expression across different cultures and time periods. From ancient cave paintings to modern digital art, the northern lights have left their glowing mark on human creativity, serving as both muse and metaphor.

The Northern Lights in Traditional Art

Many indigenous cultures in the Arctic regions have incorporated the northern lights into their artistic traditions. The Inuit, Sami, and other northern peoples have long seen the auroras as deeply spiritual, representing the presence of ancestors or divine spirits. In their art, the lights often appear as motifs of power, reverence, or natural wonder, appearing in intricate carvings, textiles, and storytelling traditions.

In Sami culture, for instance, the auroras feature prominently in their folklore and traditional handicrafts. Their colorful woven patterns often reflect the hues of the northern lights, symbolizing the connection between their people and the celestial world. Sami legends speak of the auroras as magical forces, capable of bringing both fortune and danger, depending on how they are respected.

Classical and Contemporary Painting

Throughout history, the auroras have been a subject of fascination for painters, especially during the Romantic period, when artists sought to capture the sublime power of nature.

Paintings of the northern lights by 19th-century artists like Frederic Edwin Church and Caspar David Friedrich depicted the auroras as part of a larger exploration of the human relationship with the natural world. These paintings often evoke feelings of awe and insignificance in the face of the vastness of the universe.

In more modern times, artists such as contemporary landscape painters and digital artists have continued to draw inspiration from the auroras. The rise of photography has also allowed for new interpretations of the lights, with photographers seeking to capture the movement and color of the auroras in ways that were once impossible with traditional media.

Music and the Lights: Composing Under the Aurora

The northern lights have also inspired composers and musicians. The mysterious and ever-changing nature of the auroras has often been mirrored in the structure and composition of music. For example, Jean Sibelius, the famous Finnish composer, is said to have been influenced by the northern lights while creating his symphonic works. His compositions, filled with sweeping, atmospheric sounds, seem to echo the haunting beauty of the auroras dancing across the sky.

In contemporary music, artists have drawn on the auroras as both subject matter and metaphor, creating pieces that attempt to capture the emotional and visual experience of seeing the lights. Composers of ambient and electronic music have used the auroras as inspiration for soundscapes that evoke the cold, ethereal atmosphere of the Arctic night.

Literature and Film: Telling the Story of the Lights

The northern lights have found their way into literature and film as symbols of wonder, transformation, and sometimes foreboding. In literature, the auroras are often used to represent change, spiritual journeys, or the intersection between the natural and the supernatural. In Philip Pullman's *His Dark Materials* trilogy, the auroras play a central role in the story, acting as a gateway between different worlds.

In films, the auroras have served as breathtaking backdrops and emotional catalysts. The 2019 movie *Arctic* used the northern lights to emphasize the isolation and harsh beauty of the landscape, while other films, such as *The Golden Compass*, have woven the lights into the narrative as a mystical force.

The continued presence of the auroras in art and culture speaks to their enduring power. They remain a source of inspiration, symbolizing not only the beauty of nature but also the mysteries that still linger in our universe. Whether captured in a painting, a song, or a film, the northern lights remind us that some things in the world are beyond explanation, existing purely to be marvelled at.

Chapter 12: The Auroras on other Planets

While the auroras on Earth are undoubtedly beautiful, they are not unique to our planet. In fact, the phenomenon of auroras occurs on several other planets in our solar system, creating equally stunning, yet alien, displays of light. These extraterrestrial auroras, influenced by different magnetic fields and atmospheres, offer a glimpse into the broader dynamics of the universe.

In this chapter, we'll explore the auroras of other planets, from the massive light shows on Jupiter and Saturn to the mysterious auroral activity on Mars and even some of the outer gas giants. Each planetary aurora offers new insight into the forces at work in our solar system and reminds us of the universality of this cosmic dance of light.

Jupiter's Auroras – The Giant's Light Show

Jupiter, the largest planet in our solar system, hosts some of the most spectacular auroras ever observed. Unlike Earth's auroras, which are powered primarily by solar wind, Jupiter's auroras are driven by the intense magnetic field of the planet itself. This field is about 20,000 times stronger than Earth's, and it interacts with charged particles from the planet's volcanic moon, Io, creating massive, glowing auroras at the planet's poles.

Jupiter's auroras are far more energetic than Earth's, producing X-rays as well as visible light. These auroras are so large that they could fit several Earths inside them, making them a truly awe-inspiring sight. Observed through telescopes and captured by spacecraft like NASA's Juno mission, Jupiter's auroras offer a fascinating glimpse into the power of magnetic fields in shaping planetary environments.

Saturn's Auroras – Rings of Light

Saturn, famous for its iconic rings, also experiences auroras at its poles. Like Jupiter, Saturn's auroras are influenced by its strong magnetic field, which interacts with the solar wind to create swirling displays of light. These auroras are often seen as rings of light encircling the planet's poles, much like the rings that surround the planet's equator.

Saturn's auroras are particularly striking because of their relationship to the planet's rings. When viewed together, the combination of the glowing auroras and the planet's majestic rings creates an image that seems otherworldly, a reminder that the beauty of auroras is not limited to Earth.

Mars and the Mystery of Patchy Auroras

Mars, our neighboring red planet, also experiences auroras, though they are quite different from those on Earth. Unlike Earth, Mars doesn't have a global magnetic field, but it does have localized pockets of magnetism in certain regions of the planet's crust. These magnetic pockets create small, patchy auroras that flicker across the Martian sky.

The discovery of auroras on Mars was surprising to scientists, as they didn't expect to find such activity without a global magnetic field. However, these localized auroras offer new clues about the magnetic history of Mars and its interaction with solar wind. As we continue to study the red planet, these auroras could provide important insights into the planet's past atmosphere and magnetic field.

The Auroras of Uranus and Neptune – The Outer Giants

Even the farthest planets in our solar system, Uranus and Neptune, experience auroras. However, because of their distance from the sun and the unique tilt of their magnetic fields, these auroras are far less understood than those on Earth or Jupiter. Uranus, for example, has a magnetic field that is tilted at a 60-degree angle to its axis of rotation, causing its auroras to appear in unexpected places across the planet.

Neptune, the outermost planet in the solar system, also has auroras, though they are faint and difficult to observe from Earth. Both of these ice giants offer a fascinating glimpse into how auroras form under extreme conditions, far from the influence of the sun's solar wind.

Auroras Beyond Our Solar System?

While auroras have been observed on several planets in our solar system, scientists believe that auroras may occur on exoplanets—planets orbiting other stars—as well. As we discover more exoplanets with magnetic fields and atmospheres, it's possible that future telescopes will be able to detect auroras on distant worlds.

The discovery of auroras on exoplanets would open a new chapter in our understanding of these light displays, showing us that the dance of light and magnetic energy is a universal phenomenon, occurring on planets across the galaxy.

Chapter 13: The Science Behind the Spectacle

The northern lights, or aurora borealis, may be one of the most stunning displays in nature, but beneath their beauty lies a fascinating web of physics, magnetism, and particle interactions that make this spectacle possible. In this chapter, we'll delve into the detailed science behind the auroras—how they form, why they take on certain colors, and the complex processes that govern their behavior. From the solar flares on the surface of the sun to the magnetic field that encircles Earth, every part of the northern lights is the result of interactions on a cosmic scale.

We often focus on the visible beauty of the auroras, but understanding how they are created deepens our appreciation of their complexity and wonder. Whether you're a science enthusiast or just curious about what's happening in the sky when the northern lights appear, this chapter will take you on a journey from the surface of the sun to the outer edges of Earth's atmosphere to explain what makes these lights dance across the night sky.

The Role of the Sun – The Solar Wind and Magnetic Storms

At the core of every northern light display is our sun, a giant sphere of burning plasma that powers the solar system. The northern lights begin with solar wind—streams of charged particles released from the sun's surface. This wind is made up of electrons and protons that are constantly streaming away from the sun in all directions, carried by the sun's magnetic field.

The sun is not a steady, constant star. Instead, it goes through periods of heightened activity known as solar maxima and quieter periods called solar minima. During the solar maximum, the sun's surface becomes more active, producing solar flares and coronal mass ejections (CMEs)—massive bursts of solar wind and magnetic energy. When these bursts of energy head toward Earth, they can trigger geomagnetic storms, which result in the bright, colorful displays of auroras we see.

When the solar wind reaches Earth, the planet's magnetic field acts like a shield, protecting us from most of the harmful radiation. However, at the poles, where the magnetic field is weaker, some of these particles are funneled toward Earth's atmosphere. This is where the magic happens.

Earth's Magnetic Field – A Cosmic Shield

Earth's magnetic field plays an essential role in the formation of the northern lights. This magnetic field, generated by the movement of molten iron in Earth's outer core, extends far out into space, creating a protective barrier known as the magnetosphere. The magnetosphere helps to deflect most of the solar wind, but at the magnetic poles, the field dips inward, allowing some of the solar particles to enter.

As the charged particles from the solar wind are funneled toward Earth's poles, they collide with gases in the atmosphere, primarily oxygen and nitrogen. These collisions excite the gas particles, causing them to release photons—particles of light. This is what creates the luminous colors we see during an auroral display.

The way Earth's magnetic field interacts with the solar wind creates two distinct zones of auroral activity—the auroral ovals—around the magnetic north and south poles. These ovals shift and expand during periods of heightened solar activity, allowing the lights to be seen at lower latitudes during strong geomagnetic storms.

The Colors of the Auroras

One of the most striking features of the northern lights is their vivid colors. The auroras can appear in shades of green, purple, red, blue, and even yellow. The specific colors we see depend on the type of gas particles involved and the altitude at which the collisions occur.

- **Green**: The most common color of the auroras, green is produced when solar particles collide with oxygen molecules at altitudes of about 60 to 150 miles above Earth. The green color is the result of oxygen atoms releasing energy in the form of light.

- **Red**: Red auroras are less common but equally beautiful. They occur when oxygen atoms are excited at much higher altitudes—above 150 miles. These red auroras are often faint and can appear at the top edges of a green auroral display, adding depth and complexity to the overall light show.

- **Purple and Blue**: These colors are produced by nitrogen molecules at lower altitudes. When solar particles collide with nitrogen, the resulting light can appear blue or purple, depending on the energy of the collision. These colors are often seen at the edges or bottoms of auroral curtains, especially during periods of intense geomagnetic activity.

The altitude at which the auroras form also affects their brightness and intensity. The higher the altitude, the more diffuse the light, resulting in softer, more ethereal displays. Closer to Earth, the auroras can appear brighter and more vivid, often dancing in rapid, swirling patterns across the sky.

The Role of Geomagnetic Storms

The northern lights don't simply appear as static bands of color—they move, swirl, and pulse across the sky in what can only be described as a celestial dance. This movement is the result of geomagnetic storms—disturbances in Earth's magnetic field caused by solar wind. These storms can vary in intensity, from minor disturbances to major events that cause the auroras to be visible as far south as the United States or southern Europe.

Geomagnetic storms are measured using the KP index, a scale that ranges from 0 (quiet) to 9 (major storm). The higher the KP index, the more likely it is that the auroras will be visible at lower latitudes. During strong geomagnetic storms, the auroras can cover the entire sky, stretching from horizon to horizon, with colors shifting rapidly and forming intricate patterns.

The movement of the auroras is influenced by fluctuations in the strength of the solar wind, as well as the structure of Earth's magnetic field. These factors create the swirling, curtain-like shapes that are so characteristic of the northern lights. The auroras may dance in gentle waves or flicker like flames, creating an ever-changing spectacle that can last for hours.

Space Weather and the Future of Auroras

While the northern lights are beautiful, they are also part of a larger system known as space weather. Space weather refers to the environmental conditions in space caused by the sun's activity, including solar flares, solar wind, and geomagnetic storms. Understanding space weather is important not only for predicting auroras but also for protecting our technology and infrastructure from the effects of solar storms.

During intense solar storms, the charged particles in the solar wind can interfere with satellites, GPS systems, and even power grids on Earth. In 1989, a powerful geomagnetic storm caused a blackout in Quebec, Canada, and similar storms have been known to disrupt communication systems and satellites. As we become more reliant on technology, understanding and predicting space weather becomes increasingly important.

Looking to the future, scientists are working to develop more accurate models of solar activity and space weather, allowing us to better predict when and where auroras will occur. Satellites like NASA's Solar and Heliospheric Observatory (SOHO) and the Parker Solar Probe are helping to gather data on the sun's behavior, improving our ability to forecast geomagnetic storms and protect our planet from their effects.

The Personal Experience – Standing Beneath the Lights

For all the science behind the auroras, there's nothing quite like the personal experience of standing beneath the northern lights. Whether you're a seasoned aurora chaser or a first-time viewer, witnessing the lights in person is a moment of awe and wonder. The northern lights remind us of the powerful forces at work in the universe—forces that shape our planet and connect us to the stars.

As you stand beneath the lights, it's impossible not to feel a sense of humility. The auroras are a reminder that we are just a small part of a much larger, more complex system—a system that stretches across the solar system and beyond. The lights connect us to the sun, the magnetic field, and the cosmic forces that govern the universe. And in that moment, standing beneath the swirling colors of the auroras, we are reminded of the beauty, mystery, and power of nature.

Chapter 14: The Impact on Mental Health

While the northern lights are often admired for their aesthetic beauty and scientific intrigue, many people find that the experience of watching the auroras has a profound effect on their mental health and overall well-being. In recent years, there has been growing interest in understanding how nature-based experiences, such as viewing the northern lights, can promote emotional healing, reduce stress, and foster a sense of connection and mindfulness.

This chapter explores the therapeutic benefits of witnessing the auroras and delves into how such an extraordinary natural phenomenon can influence the mind and spirit. From relieving the mental burden of stress to inspiring creativity and self-reflection, the northern lights are more than just a visual spectacle—they are a source of emotional transformation.

The Healing Power of the Auroras

Numerous studies have shown that spending time in nature has significant benefits for mental health, ranging from reducing stress and anxiety to boosting mood and fostering a sense of peace. This concept is often referred to as "nature therapy" or "ecotherapy." The northern lights, as a unique and awe-inspiring aspect of the natural world, are particularly powerful in triggering these positive effects.

Being in the presence of the auroras often evokes a sense of awe—a complex emotional response that blends feelings of wonder, admiration, and humility. Awe-inspiring experiences, such as witnessing the northern lights, have been shown to increase feelings of happiness and contentment, while also reducing the focus on everyday worries. Researchers have found that awe can alter a person's perception of time, leading to feelings of expansiveness and helping individuals feel more connected to the world around them.

Additionally, awe-inducing experiences can lower levels of cortisol, the body's primary stress hormone, leading to a more relaxed state of mind. This helps to alleviate stress, promote mindfulness, and create a sense of mental clarity that can last long after the lights have faded from the sky.

The Power of Awe and Mindfulness

One of the most fascinating psychological effects of seeing the northern lights is the power of awe. Awe is a transformative emotion that encourages people to shift their focus from their individual concerns to a broader, more collective perspective. Standing beneath the northern lights, one cannot help but feel small in comparison to the vastness of the universe, which often brings about a deep sense of humility.

Awe experiences also encourage mindfulness—the practice of being fully present in the moment. In our fast-paced, technology-driven world, people often struggle to disconnect from the constant stream of notifications, tasks, and worries. However, the northern lights demand full attention. The lights' unpredictable movements, shifting colors, and fleeting presence create a moment that is both beautiful and ephemeral. This encourages viewers to focus on the present, heightening their awareness and connection to the natural world around them.

For many people, aurora watching becomes a form of meditation, a time to quiet the mind and be fully immersed in the experience. This mindfulness can carry over into everyday life, helping individuals approach challenges with a calmer, more centered mindset.

Creativity and Inspiration – Fuel for the Imagination

Throughout history, the northern lights have been a source of inspiration for artists, writers, musicians, and other creatives. From ancient myths and folklore to modern photography and digital art, the auroras have fueled the imagination of countless people across the world. This is because the experience of seeing the northern lights activates areas of the brain associated with creativity and problem-solving.

Awe and inspiration are closely linked. When people are exposed to awe-inspiring experiences, such as watching the auroras, their minds tend to open up to new possibilities. This mental shift encourages creativity, allowing individuals to think more expansively and come up with innovative ideas. Artists often describe the northern lights as a muse, with the ethereal beauty of the lights sparking new ideas and projects.

Writers and poets are similarly drawn to the northern lights as a metaphor for transformation, mystery, and the unknown. The fleeting nature of the auroras, combined with their otherworldly appearance, has made them a powerful symbol in literature, representing everything from the cycle of life and death to the presence of divine forces.

Even if you're not an artist or a writer, witnessing the northern lights can inspire creative thinking in everyday life. The experience can help you break free from rigid thought patterns, approach problems from new angles, and find creative solutions to challenges.

Reducing Anxiety and Depression through Connection with Nature

In a world where anxiety and depression are increasingly common, reconnecting with nature has been shown to be an effective way to improve mental well-being. Viewing the northern lights, with their calming movements and vibrant colors, can have a particularly powerful effect on those struggling with mental health challenges.

For many people, the northern lights evoke a sense of connection—both to the natural world and to something larger than themselves. This connection can foster feelings of peace and acceptance, helping individuals to step back from their daily stresses and gain perspective on their problems. In this way, viewing the auroras becomes a form of emotional release, allowing people to let go of their anxieties and reconnect with the beauty of life.

Moreover, the act of waiting for the northern lights to appear encourages patience, mindfulness, and resilience. Aurora watching often requires long periods of standing in the cold, scanning the skies for signs of activity. This can be a meditative process in itself, teaching individuals the value of patience and persistence—lessons that are applicable not only to aurora chasing but also to managing stress and emotional challenges in everyday life.

In some cases, simply being in the presence of the auroras can provide emotional comfort. The slow, rhythmic dance of the lights creates a calming effect, while the vivid greens, purples, and reds inspire a sense of joy and wonder. For those suffering from depression, such experiences can offer a break from feelings of hopelessness, even if just for a short while.

The Social Aspect – Shared Experiences and Community

One often overlooked aspect of aurora chasing is the social connection that comes with it. Whether you're traveling with friends or family or meeting fellow aurora chasers along the way, the shared experience of witnessing the northern lights can strengthen social bonds and create a sense of community.

There's something magical about sharing the moment when the lights appear—watching as the sky shifts and pulses with color, standing in awe alongside others who are equally mesmerized. This sense of shared wonder brings people closer together, creating lasting memories and strengthening relationships.

For many, the journey to see the northern lights is also an opportunity to meet like-minded individuals who share a passion for nature, adventure, and exploration. Whether at aurora lodges, on guided tours, or through online communities, aurora chasers often form connections with others who understand the thrill of seeing the lights and the patience required to wait for them. These connections can be deeply meaningful, offering a sense of camaraderie and belonging.

Lasting Effects – The Emotional Afterglow

The emotional impact of witnessing the northern lights doesn't end when the lights disappear. For many people, the experience leaves a lasting "afterglow"—a sense of peace, happiness, and fulfillment that can linger for days, weeks, or even longer. This emotional afterglow often leads to a renewed appreciation for life's beauty and a deeper sense of gratitude for the natural world.

People who experience the northern lights often describe a feeling of renewal, as if the lights have touched something deep within them. The sense of awe and wonder they inspire can lead to greater emotional resilience, helping individuals cope with life's challenges in a more balanced and mindful way.

For those lucky enough to witness the lights multiple times, each experience can be different, offering new perspectives and emotions. Whether it's the colors, the movement, or the shared moments with others, every auroral display has the potential to be a deeply transformative experience.

Conclusion: The Universal Dance

From the frozen landscapes of the Arctic Circle to the distant planets of our solar system, the northern lights remind us of the awe-inspiring beauty that the universe holds. As we've journeyed through the myths, science, art, and personal experiences surrounding the aurora borealis, we've uncovered just a glimpse of the rich legacy these lights have bestowed upon humanity.

At the heart of the northern lights is a reminder that our world—and the universe beyond it—is still full of mystery. In an era where technology brings us closer to understanding the stars, where we can map distant galaxies and send probes to the edges of the solar system, the auroras remain something that cannot be entirely predicted or controlled. Their unpredictability is part of their charm and magic, drawing us into the age-old dance of light and shadow across the sky.

The auroras serve as both a scientific phenomenon and a symbol of the human experience. For millennia, people have looked up at these lights and interpreted them through the lens of their cultures, beliefs, and spiritual understanding. The Vikings saw them as reflections of armour-clad Valkyries, while the Inuit envisioned the souls of ancestors playing games in the heavens. Today, we still marvel at the lights, blending science with our enduring sense of wonder. Whether we approach them through the lens of physics or folklore, the northern lights continue to resonate deeply in our hearts and minds.

As we have explored, the northern lights are more than just an Earthly event—they are a cosmic display, occurring on other planets, each with its own distinct characteristics and beauty. The study of auroras beyond Earth shows us that these lights are not confined to our world. They are a universal phenomenon, powered by the same forces of solar winds and magnetic fields that shape planets and stars across the galaxy. From the swirling rings of light on Jupiter to the flickering, patchy auroras of Mars, we are reminded that this cosmic display is a shared feature of planetary systems—a universal dance across the universe.

Yet, as timeless as they feel, the future of the northern lights may not be as certain as we'd like to believe. Climate change and increasing light pollution threaten the pristine environments from which these lights are best observed. The Arctic is warming at an unprecedented rate, potentially changing the landscape and cloud cover that allow us to witness the lights so clearly. Cities are expanding, their lights encroaching on areas that were once bathed only in the glow of the auroras.

It is crucial that we become stewards of these environments. The preservation of dark skies and cold, clear nights is essential if we want future generations to experience the magic of the aurora borealis. Reducing light pollution, supporting dark sky reserves, and practicing sustainable travel are small but important steps toward ensuring that these natural wonders remain accessible.

In addition to the environmental challenges, we must also be mindful of how human technology might affect auroral activity. As space tourism and satellite constellations increase, we need to consider the long-term impact of human-made light and electromagnetic interference on the visibility of the auroras. Our pursuit of technological advancement should not come at the cost of one of the most profound natural phenomena we are fortunate enough to witness.

For those who have stood beneath the northern lights, the experience is nothing short of transformative. It's not just about the spectacle—it's about feeling connected to something larger, something ancient and infinite. The auroras remind us that, despite the hustle of modern life, we are still part of a larger cosmic story. They pull us out of our daily concerns and root us in a moment of pure beauty, where time seems to slow, and the only thing that matters is the dance of light above us.

As we conclude this exploration of the magic and mystery of the northern lights, we leave with a deeper appreciation for the beauty, fragility, and universality of this phenomenon. Whether you've seen the auroras in person, dream of doing so, or simply admire them from afar, let the lights remind you of the incredible wonders that still exist in the world—and the universe—around us. They are more than just lights in the sky; they are a testament to the forces that shape planets, guide stars, and connect us all in the vastness of space.

The northern lights are, and always will be, a symbol of the unknown and the unexplainable. They show us that, no matter how much we learn about the world and the universe, there will always be moments that leave us in awe—moments that humble us, inspire us, and remind us that the universe is far greater than we can ever truly comprehend.

As long as the northern lights continue to dance, we, too, are invited to be part of this celestial performance. In every flicker of green, every swirl of purple, and every burst of red, the auroras offer us a glimpse of the extraordinary. And for that, we should be forever grateful.

So, as you move forward, may the lights guide you. May they remind you to look up, to wonder, and to cherish the magic that exists both in the skies above and in the hearts of those who dream.

Epilogue

As we come to the close of this journey through the magic and mystery of the northern lights, it's important to reflect not just on the science, stories, and experiences we've explored, but on the deeper meaning these lights hold for each of us. The northern lights are much more than a natural phenomenon; they are a reminder of the wonder, beauty, and connection that exist in the universe. Their fleeting presence in the night sky serves as a powerful metaphor for the delicate balance of life, and they leave an impression that lingers long after they have faded from sight.

For centuries, humans have sought meaning in the northern lights. Whether as omens, spiritual symbols, or signs from the heavens, the auroras have always invoked a sense of something greater than us. In today's world, that sense of wonder remains intact. Even though we have a scientific understanding of the northern lights, knowing how they form and why they appear does little to diminish their awe-inspiring power. In fact, understanding the cosmic forces that create the auroras can deepen our appreciation for the intricate, interconnected systems that govern our planet and the universe beyond.

In this epilogue, let us contemplate the lessons the northern lights offer us—about life, about nature, and about ourselves. From their unpredictability to their transformative power, the auroras are more than just lights in the sky—they are a source of inspiration, reflection, and hope. They remind us of the enduring mysteries of the universe and our place within it.

Embracing the Unknown

Perhaps one of the most significant lessons the northern lights teach us is the value of embracing the unknown. The auroras are notoriously unpredictable, appearing when conditions align and disappearing just as quickly. For many aurora chasers, this uncertainty is part of the allure. Waiting for the lights requires patience, persistence, and acceptance of the fact that nature follows its own rules.

In life, much like when chasing the northern lights, we are often faced with the unknown. We cannot predict everything that will happen, nor can we control every outcome. The northern lights remind us that sometimes, the most beautiful and meaningful experiences come from moments of uncertainty. It's in these moments—when we let go of expectations and embrace the unknown—that we find magic, whether it's in the sky or in our lives.

Learning to appreciate the unknown allows us to approach life with greater openness and curiosity. It teaches us to savor the present moment, to recognize that beauty can arise when we least expect it, and to trust that some things are simply beyond our control. The northern lights are a perfect example of how something fleeting and elusive can hold immense power and meaning, reminding us to find peace in the unpredictability of life.

Finding Beauty in Ephemerality

The northern lights are a fleeting spectacle, often lasting only minutes or hours before they vanish into the darkness. Their transitory nature is part of what makes them so captivating. They appear, dance across the sky, and then disappear, leaving us with the memory of their beauty. This ephemeral quality forces us to be fully present in the moment, to appreciate the lights while they last.

In a broader sense, the northern lights teach us about the importance of finding beauty in life's ephemeral moments. Much like the auroras, the most precious moments in life are often short-lived—an unexpected laugh, a stunning sunset, a heartfelt conversation. These moments may pass quickly, but their impact can last a lifetime. The northern lights remind us to cherish these fleeting experiences, to hold onto the joy and wonder they bring, even as they fade.

The lesson of ephemerality is also a reminder that nothing in life is permanent. Change is inevitable, and just as the northern lights come and go, so too do the experiences, challenges, and joys of life. Learning to appreciate the temporary nature of life's moments can help us cultivate gratitude and mindfulness, allowing us to fully engage with the world around us.

Connection to Something Greater

For many who witness the northern lights, the experience is more than just a visual feast—it's a spiritual or emotional awakening. The vastness of the sky, the brilliance of the lights, and the knowledge that this phenomenon is the result of forces far beyond our understanding can evoke a profound sense of connection to something greater than ourselves.

This sense of connection is a key aspect of the human experience. Whether we define it as a connection to nature, the cosmos, or a higher power, the feeling of being part of something much larger than ourselves brings a sense of peace and perspective. The northern lights, with their grandeur and mystery, remind us of our place in the universe—that we are just a small part of an enormous, interconnected system.

In the presence of the northern lights, many people feel a sense of humility. The lights stretch across the sky, indifferent to our worries and concerns, existing on a scale and timeline far beyond our own. Yet, despite this humbling realization, the northern lights also remind us that we are part of this grand system. We are connected to the same cosmic forces that create the auroras, and in that connection, we find a sense of belonging and purpose.

A Source of Hope and Wonder

In a world that can often feel overwhelming or uncertain, the northern lights offer a source of hope and wonder. They remind us that there is still beauty in the world, that there are forces at play that inspire awe and curiosity. The lights are a reminder that, despite the challenges we face, there are moments of magic that can lift our spirits and renew our sense of wonder.

Hope is an essential aspect of the human experience. It drives us to keep moving forward, to look for beauty and meaning even in difficult times. The northern lights are a symbol of this hope— a reminder that even in the darkest, coldest nights, the sky can light up with beauty and joy. They teach us to hold onto hope, to keep looking up, and to believe that something wonderful might be just around the corner.

The northern lights also encourage us to maintain a sense of wonder. In a world where so much is known and explained, the auroras remind us that there are still mysteries to be explored, still moments of awe to be experienced. Wonder keeps us curious, keeps us striving to learn more and experience more. It's what drives us to explore the world, to chase the lights, and to seek out beauty in all its forms.

Carrying the Experience Forward

The memory of witnessing the northern lights stays with those who are lucky enough to see them. Long after the lights have faded from the sky, the emotional and spiritual impact of the experience lingers. For many, it's a moment of profound connection—to nature, to the universe, and to themselves.

Carrying this experience forward means holding onto the lessons the northern lights teach us—lessons of patience, mindfulness, connection, and wonder. It means taking the sense of awe and beauty we felt beneath the lights and applying it to our everyday lives, finding magic in the small, fleeting moments that make life extraordinary.

Whether you've seen the northern lights once or many times, or whether you still dream of witnessing them one day, their impact goes far beyond the visual display. They are a reminder of the beauty that exists in the world and within ourselves. The lights encourage us to keep looking up, to keep seeking out wonder and connection, and to remember that we are part of a much larger, more mysterious universe.

As you close the pages of this book, may you carry with you the lessons of the northern lights. Let them guide you through moments of uncertainty, inspire you in times of creativity, and remind you to find beauty in the fleeting moments of life. The auroras may be ephemeral, but their impact is lasting—a testament to the magic and mystery that still exists in our world.

Keep looking up. The lights will always be there, dancing in the sky, waiting to remind you of the wonder that surrounds us all.